TERMINAL
Living

A CALL TO
LIVE A LIFE
BEYOND LIMITS

Dr. Sandy Madden

TERMINAL LIVING
© 2012 Sandra Madden

Scripture quotations marked AMP are taken from the Amplified® Bible, Copyright © 1954, 1958, 1962, 1964, 1965, 1987 by The Lockman Foundation. Used by permission." (www.Lockman.org) Scripture quotations marked NLT are taken from the Holy Bible, New Living Translation, copyright © 1996, 2004. Used by permission of Tyndale House Publishers, Inc., Wheaton, Illinois 60189. All rights reserved. Scripture quotations marked NKJV are taken from the New King James Version®. Copyright © 1982 by Thomas Nelson, Inc. Used by permission. All rights reserved. Scriptures marked as CEV are taken from the Contemporary English Version, Second Edition, Copyright © 2006 by American Bible Society. Used by permission. All rights reserved. Scriptures marked as MSG are taken from The Message. Copyright © 1993, 1994, 1995, 1996, 2000, 2001, 2002. Used by permission of NavPress Publishing Group. Scriptures marked NIV are taken from the Holy Bible, NEW INTERNATIONAL VERSION®. Copyright © 1973, 1978, 1984 by Biblica, Inc. All rights reserved worldwide. Used by permission

WORD ALIVE PRESS
Just Write!

Word Alive Press
131 Cordite Road, Winnipeg, MB R3W 1S1
www.wordalivepress.ca

Printed in Canada

Library and Archives Canada Cataloguing in Publication

Madden, Sandy, 1964-
    Terminal Living: A Call to Live a Life Beyond Limits / Sandy Madden.

Includes bibliographical references.
ISBN 978-1-77069-434-7

1. Self-actualization (Psychology). 2. Death.
3. Conduct of life. 4. Quality of life. I. Title.

BF637.34M33185 2012   158.1   C2011-907824-4

.

CONTENTS

To my best friend and husband, George – for being my greatest inspiration and encourager.

I also want to express my heartfelt gratitude to my mentor for this project, Judy Rushfeldt. The many hours you spent on proofing, advising and guiding me step by step were invaluable. May the wisdom and passion you so freely gave return to you in multiplied fashion.

INTRODUCTION

This book began almost five years ago after an event that radically altered our family's life. What happened as a result of this event has irrevocably changed our perspective about life, caused us to re-evaluate our priorities, and redirected our goals.

My husband George and I were empty nesters, contentedly pursuing successful careers and enjoying mid-life with all our material needs well provided. One phone call shattered this blissful bubble in an instant—George's brother had died.

Dale was George's elder by three years and was only fifty-one when his life was cut short. His death brought us face to face with the stark reality that life is not a dress rehearsal. It became startlingly clear that we only had one opportunity to enjoy our life and invest in the relationships and pursuits that matter most.

The dismal truth is that we are all going to die. None of us have a guarantee of tomorrow. Terminal living means recognizing the brevity of life and making the most of what you've been given. By definition, terminal living doesn't mean satisfying every whim or fancy, but directing our energies and passions towards something greater than ourselves.

It is not simply, "Eat, drink and be merry for tomorrow we may die," which implies a narcissistic approach to life. Rather it is, "Pursue personal growth, invest in others, and bequeath your passion to the next generation for tomorrow we will die." Life in this context is elevated to a new level of purpose and fulfillment.

This book is birthed out of my personal journey through a time of great conflict, pain and struggle and my desire to help others on a similar quest. As I've walked through the often challenging process of growth and change, I've drawn strength from others who have blazed the trail ahead of me. One such person was Terry Fox (1958–1981).

Terry was diagnosed with cancer at the age of nineteen while he was attending University. Doctors informed him that his leg had to be amputated and that his treatment would also require chemotherapy. Terry was impressed that because of advances made in cancer research he was given a fifty percent chance of survival, when only two years previously it would have been just fifteen percent.

Through his gruelling sixteen months of treatment, Terry maintained a positive attitude. His optimistic mindset contributed to a rapid recovery and after only three weeks he was walking on his artificial leg and soon playing golf. However, Terry's heart went out to his fellow cancer patients who were not so fortunate, and he became determined to do whatever he could to bring courage to them.

Terry decided to embark on a cross-country marathon, through which he hoped to raise a million dollars for cancer research. He sent a letter requesting financial support to the Canadian Cancer Society on October 15, 1979, which outlined his courageous intent to "conquer" his disability and to finish his run even if it meant he had to "crawl every last mile." In the letter, Terry also described the indelible mark left on him by the people who were undergoing cancer treatment with him:

> There were faces with the brave smiles, and the ones who had given up smiling. There were feelings of hopeful denial, and the feelings of despair. My quest would not be a selfish one. I could not leave knowing these faces and feelings would still exist, even though I would be set free from mine. Somewhere the hurting must stop...and I was determined to take myself to the limit for this cause.[1]

As a true champion of terminal living, Terry stated, "I remember promising myself that, should I live, I would rise up to meet this new challenge [of fundraising for cancer research] face to face and prove myself worthy of life, something too many people take for granted."[1]

Unfortunately, about one third of the way across Canada, Terry was forced to stop running. Cancer finally overcame his body and he died on June 28, 1981, at the age of twenty-three. Fox never made his goal of physically crossing the nation, but his spirit and his courage did. He surpassed his goal to raise a million dollars for cancer research as money poured in from all over the country, reaching a staggering twenty-three million.

Addressing the House of Commons, Prime Minister Trudeau said of Terry, "It occurs very rarely in the life of a nation that the courageous spirit of one person unites all people in the celebration of his life and in the mourning of his death…We do not think of him as one who was defeated by misfortune but as one who inspired us with the example of the triumph of the human spirit over adversity."[2]

Terry Fox was the epitome of terminal living. The fullness of his life came from his fearless comprehension and defiance of death. The expectation of his death did not discourage him but rather fuelled his passion for life. He wanted to make every moment count. He saw beyond the pain and the limits of his failing body to those who would benefit by his sacrifice. He knew his body would only be here a short time but he understood his spirit would live on in the hearts of those who were touched by his life.

Whatever challenge you may be facing, this book is filled with real life stories of people who have learned to conquer adversity, rise above mediocrity and live life on a higher plane. It is my sincere desire to inspire you to live this kind of amazing life—a terminal life.

1

TIME IS TICKING

DANNY SAT IN numbed silence, staring in disbelief at the lifeless body of his beloved wife, Alicia. Scrambled thoughts cascaded through his tortured mind—"She was only fifty-two..."—"So many things left un-done..."—"So many words left unspoken..."—"Why did she have to leave so soon?"

Bereft and confused, Danny was faced with a life-altering decision—to retreat into self-pity, regret and bitterness or to stir up the dying embers of his own dreams so that he could do all the things he said one day he would.

Death has a way of putting everything in proper perspective. Movies like *The Bucket List*, and songs like, *Live like You Were Dying*, are portraits of the essence of terminal living—catalyzing life through the knowledge of death.

However, it's crucial to grasp that we don't need to wait till we get "the news" that we're dying before we begin to really live the life we always dreamed. Let me give you a newsflash—all of us have already received "the news." We are all going to die. The question is—are we going to really live while we have the chance?

Terminal Living

That's what terminal living is all about—living life at its best—to the full. People are often justifiably concerned about whether there is life after death. But the question we need to ask and examine today is—"Will there be life before death?" That's terminal living.

AVERAGE LIFE EXPECTANCY

Sometimes complacency—the enemy of terminal living—settles on us like a dense fog that clouds our vision and saps our passion. We need the stark light of reality to penetrate the haze in order for us to comprehend the gravity of our condition. The purpose of the statistics below is to awaken your slumbering passion, heighten your dissatisfaction with the status quo, and cause you to shake off complacency so you can experience life at a higher level.

> If you are thirty-seven, your life is half over.

A recent report stated that the average life expectancy of North Americans had risen to 80.4 years from 77.8 years in the previous year's study. However, the same report revealed that the actual average age of death was only 74.2 years.[3]

To speak generously, the average North American has about seventy-five years to live. This may sound like a long time, especially to someone who is twenty-five or younger. However, for those who have passed into later adulthood, seventy-five may seem all too close at hand. To put it in perspective, if you are thirty-seven, your life is half over. If you are fifty, your life is two-thirds of the way over. This news can either depress you or motivate you, depending on your point of view.

WHERE DOES THE TIME GO?

If you still feel like you have all the time in the world, consider the following startling facts.

If you're like most people, who work eight hours a day and retire at sixty-five, you will have invested approximately eleven years of your life into your occupation. The average person sleeps about eight hours each night. Understanding that there are twenty-four hours in a day, you can calculate that you sleep one-third of your life away. This means the average seventy-five-year-old has spent twenty-five years sleeping. If you graduate from high school and attend just two years of post-secondary training, you will have invested approximately five years of your life into education.

The results of a recent survey say that the average American watches at least four hours of television per day. Over a sixty-five-year lifespan, that translates into more than thirteen years being lost to television.[4]

If you total the years spent simply watching television, working, going to school, and sleeping, you will have spent almost fifty-five of your seventy-five years. The bulk of the remaining twenty years are sucked up with endless everyday activities which can include, but are not limited to:

- driving to and from appointments, sporting activities, social functions, and work.
- personal hygiene, fitness, and cosmetic treatments.
- cleaning and maintaining your house, vehicles, toys, and property.
- talking on the phone, being put on hold, and texting.
- waiting in doctors' offices, lawyers' offices, banks, and line-ups of every description.
- shopping for groceries, clothes, school supplies, and other necessities.
- preparing, eating, and cleaning up after meals.
- surfing the Internet, particularly on Facebook and other social network sites.

A recent survey states:

In a monthly view of U.S. Internet activity for top parent companies and web brands, The Nielsen Company found that the average time users spend using Facebook per month grew nearly 10%, topping seven hours. Additionally, the number of those actively using the web grew 3.8%, to slightly more than 203 million users.[5]

All of these statistics should hopefully awaken us to the reality of how precious our time really is. How often have we said, "Someday, I'm going to learn to play the guitar, take art classes, take my spouse on a nice holiday, spend more time with my kids, etc...."? The truth is that we don't have that many "somedays."

TIME PAST

This problem is not new to humanity. Contrary to many who blame all our woes on the vices of modern living, history records the words of those who experienced the very same limitations of time. Seneca, a Roman philosopher who lived in the first century AD made this statement:

> We all sorely complain of the shortness of time, and yet have much more than we know what to do with. Our lives are either spent in doing nothing at all, or in doing nothing to the purpose, or in doing nothing that we ought to do. We are always complaining that our days are few, and acting as though there would be no end of them.[6]

Even further back in history, during the seventh century BC, King David of Israel said, *"Teach us to realize the brevity of life, so that we may grow in wisdom."*[7]

Deep in the heart of every person, there is something which acknowledges that this earthly existence cannot be all there is to life. We are all driven by an inherent desire to experience life beyond the limits of time. The wisest and richest man who ever lived, King Solomon, recorded it this way:

> He [God] also has planted eternity in men's hearts
> and minds [a divinely implanted sense of a purpose
> working through the ages which nothing under the
> sun but God alone can satisfy].[8]

Mankind is on an endless quest for eternal life. Ancient myths speak of the fountain of youth and the holy grail, while modern fantasies have turned to the ideas of cryogenics and even time travel. Early cultures followed elaborate customs and rituals in feeble attempts to immortalize themselves. The Egyptians built pyramids, the Mayans built temples, and the Chinese buried their emperors with entire armies, all in an effort to extend their transitory lives beyond the realm of time and stretch into the eternal.

Unfortunately, no matter what mankind attempts in order to elude death, he is inevitably faced with the inescapable reality of time and the cessation of life. The Psalmist wrote, *"The life of mortals is like grass, they flourish like a flower of the field; the wind blows over it and it is gone, and its place remembers it no more."*[9]

In Western Canada, where I live, you can walk through a meadow in the spring and see the most colorful array of blooming wildflowers. The first flower to emerge is the crocus, a beautiful soft purple flower that bravely blooms while the snow is still on the ground. Its delicate petals signal the end of winter and the beginning of spring. These elegant heralds seem to spring up overnight and can cover an entire hillside.

But just as suddenly as they appear, they shrivel and are no more.

However, while these tiny flowers live they bring great joy in anticipation of the warmth and new life of spring. Though they enjoy only a short existence, they cheerfully fulfill their purpose and magnificently announce the arrival of spring. Our lives are similar. We have just a short time to bloom. We must use what time we have to bring purpose to our lives and joy to the world around us.

Time, not money, is the only universal currency of the earth. Time is what we trade to obtain money, friendship, and every other thing we desire. We trade our time for the things we value most. Each man is given the freedom to choose how he will invest his time. Like water on dry ground, once it is spilled it cannot be recovered, but it will produce a harvest. Wisdom teaches us to pour our time into pursuits that will blossom into things of beauty.

Carl Sandburg, a three-time Pulitzer-Prize-winning author, confirmed the crucial nature of time when he said, "Time is the coin of your life. It is the only coin you have, and only you can determine how it will be spent. Be careful lest you let other people spend it for you."[10]

> **Time, not money, is the only universal currency of the earth.**

International speaker and author Michael Le-Boeuf also wisely advised: "Waste your money and you're only out of money, but waste your time and you've lost a part of your life."[11]

The quality of our lives will be determined by the quality of the time we spend.

2

FORGOTTEN DREAMS

CHILDHOOD DREAMS

CHILDHOOD WAS A wonderful time when we imagined ourselves as conquering heroes, royal princesses and adventurous explorers. Our dreams knew no limits and carried our little hearts to the highest heights of wonder and anticipation of the world we would create.

"When I grow up I'm going to..." was the confident declaration of our innocence. However, as life began to unfold, many of us gradually came to the realization that we were grown up and that our lives were not turning out as we had hoped.

These moments of self-awareness are vital to terminal living. It is at these crossroads that we are offered the opportunity to resign ourselves to our current direction and forget our dreams or make a choice to embark on a new path that will carry us towards them.

Sir Francis Bacon once said, "They are ill discoverers that think there is no land, when they can see nothing but sea."[12]

As we sail through life and all that seems to greet our bleary gaze is an endless grey and stormy sea, it is easy to feel like we will never reach that distant and elusive shore. Yet it is exactly then that we must not cast our dreams overboard. Instead we must employ our dreams as our compass to guide us through the raging waters safely to our journey's end.

A rock is just a rock until someone with a dream looks at it. Michelangelo said, "I saw the angel in the marble and carved until I set him free."[13] When we are born, our dreamy eyes can envision our lives being any number of beautiful, magical things. We cannot allow the difficulties of life to cloud our vision to the beauty hidden within the common and even unattractive parts of our lives. The dream is still there, just waiting for us to begin carving and to set it free.

JOSEPH THE DREAMER

History is full of people who had dreams that seemed impossible to achieve. Around the year 1,400 BC, there was a young boy named Joseph who had a childhood dream. He dreamed of one day being a great king who would rule over the whole world. He was the tenth and much-loved son of a wealthy nomadic chief.

Joseph's stepbrothers were jealous of the special favor their father showed him, but they despised him even more for his dream. It was bad enough that he was his father's favorite, but now he thought he would rule over them. In ancient Middle Eastern culture, the eldest son would be granted pre-eminence in the family—certainly not the tenth-born. In their resentment,

Joseph's brothers devised a plan to rid themselves of this dreamer. They initially planned to kill him, but instead they sold him to a slave trader and deceived their father into believing a wild animal had killed Joseph.

The story of their treachery is recorded in the book of Genesis:

> When Joseph's brothers saw him coming, they recognized him in the distance. As he approached, they made plans to kill him. "Here comes the dreamer!" they said. "Come on, let's kill him and throw him into one of these cisterns. We can tell our father, 'a wild animal has eaten him.' Then we'll see what becomes of his dreams!"[14]

When you examine the brothers' words, it is evident that their hatred for Joseph grew out of their scorn for his dreams. They wanted to destroy him and his dreams. They realized after some discussion that it wasn't necessary to actually kill Joseph to destroy him. They understood that if they simply destroyed his dream they would destroy the boy.

Joseph's brothers represent what life does with many of us as we grow older. Our childhood dreams are destroyed by life's disappointments, abuse, betrayal, frustration, loss, and pain. Time itself seems to slowly erode our dreams as relentlessly as the pounding surf does the shoreline.

American actor John Barrymore once accurately stated, "A man is not old until regrets take the place of dreams."[15]

For almost two decades, Joseph endured enslavement, false accusations, imprisonment, abandonment, rejection, loneliness, and fear. Many nights he must have wondered, "Will I ever see my dream come true? Maybe it was just a youthful fantasy like my brothers told me."

In spite of all that life threw at him, Joseph kept his attitude positive and worked diligently as he carried the dream imperceptibly in his heart. Seventeen years later, the dream came to fulfillment as his brothers and his entire family bowed before him as the ruler of Egypt, second only to Pharaoh himself.

When the family was reunited, Joseph showed no resentment for what his brothers had done:

> Joseph told them to come closer to him, and when they did, he said: "Yes, I am your brother Joseph, the one you sold into Egypt. Don't worry or blame yourselves for what you did. God is the one who sent me ahead of you to save lives. But God sent me on ahead of you to keep your families alive and to save you in this wonderful way. After all, you weren't really the ones who sent me here—it was God. He made me the highest official in the king's court and placed me over all Egypt."[16]

Joseph's gracious words revealed he understood a key to achieving your dreams: there is no person and no circumstance that can stop you from realizing your dreams. The rocks thrown at you can either become your stumbling blocks or your building blocks. You cannot control what happens to you, but you can control how you respond.

The story of Joseph may sound inspiring but too good to be true. That was a long time ago. His dreams may have come true, but what about yours? In light of all the disillusionments of life, is it even realistic to hold on to your childhood dreams? Or are they simply fantasies? Those who have given up on dreaming will tell you you're wasting your time. But there are still people today who dare to dream and who actually live their dreams. One such person was Randy Pausch.

> **There is no person and no circumstance that can stop you from realizing your dreams.**

RANDY PAUSCH

Randy Pausch (1960–2008) was an extraordinary man who lived a terminal life. As a computer science professor at Carnegie Mellon University in Pittsburgh, Pennsylvania, he imparted his passion for life and left an indelible mark on his students.

At age forty-six, Randy was diagnosed with pancreatic cancer and given only three to six months of good health left to enjoy. Refusing to be paralyzed by fear and bitterness, he lived a life that was an inspiration to others. On September 18, 2007, he gave his renowned lecture titled *The Last Lecture: Really Achieving Your Childhood Dreams.* He subsequently co-authored a book by the same title, which became a New York Times best-seller.[17] Cancer finally claimed Randy's body two years after his original diagnosis, but even death could not steal the undying contribution of his terminal life.[18]

During his Last Lecture on September 18, 2007, Randy said:

> Almost all of us have childhood dreams; for example, being an astronaut, or making movies or video games for a living. Sadly, most people don't achieve theirs, and I think that's a shame. I had several specific childhood dreams, and I've actually achieved most of them. More importantly, I have found ways... of helping many young people actually achieve their childhood dreams.[19]

Randy didn't wait till he found out he had three months to live before he began pursuing his childhood dreams. He understood the power of living a terminal life. From the days of his youth till he died, he lived each day to the full and looked for opportunities to invest in the lives and dreams of others.

A major key that helped Randy achieve his dreams was that he never lost sight of them through the hard times. He had this to say about setbacks:

But remember, the brick walls are there for a reason. The brick walls are not there to keep us out. The brick walls are there to give us a chance to show how badly we want something. Because the brick walls are there to stop the people who don't want it badly enough. They're there to stop the other people.... brick walls let us show our dedication. They are there to separate us from the people who don't really want to achieve their childhood dreams. Don't bail. The best of the gold's at the bottom of barrels of crap.[20]

The question remains: how bad do you want to achieve your dreams? Are you willing to climb the brick walls that stand in your way? Are you willing to dive into the "barrels of crap" to get the gold?

Many times people have told my husband and me that they want to have our life. People see us living our dreams and think they want the same dream. They only see the "gold." They didn't see us when we were covered in "crap," scrambling over brick walls to achieve our dreams. My husband often says, "If you want what we have, then you need to be willing to do what we did to get it." That's usually when people walk away. They don't want it badly enough.

Theodore Roosevelt was the twenty-sixth and one of the greatest presidents of the United States. He was an unhealthy child who suffered from asthma. Yet he did not allow his condition to limit him. He was determined to push his weakened body to the limits of an aggressive lifestyle. He enjoyed a wide variety of interests, and accomplished many things through his renowned enthusiastic personality. He was regarded as a man's man and exuded a "cowboy" image. He became the first American to win the Nobel Prize and the youngest US president in history. Roosevelt's policies were characterized by his slogan, "Speak softly and carry a big stick."[21]

No stranger to working hard to achieve a dream, Roosevelt wisely affirmed: "Far and away the best prize that life has to offer is the chance to work hard at work worth doing."[22]

> "Opportunity is missed by most people because it is dressed in overalls and looks like work."

The great American inventor, Thomas Edison, understood that dreams were not realized without a great deal of effort. He is credited with the statement: "Opportunity is missed by most people because it is dressed in overalls and looks like work."[23]

You may be at a crossroads right now, wondering if it's possible to achieve your dreams. The lives of Theodore Rooseveldt, Randy Pausch, and Joseph tell you that with some persistence, it is. Terminal living is what will empower you to do it. Keep your eyes on the prize. Focus. Don't let a little opposition or hard work make you throw in the towel.

3

THE LAND OF GOOD INTENTIONS

PETER MARSHALL

PETER MARSHALL (1902–1949) WAS a Scottish clergy-
man who left his homeland at age twenty-four to pursue a call to the United States. Despite a lack of
money, he attended seminary and upon graduation
established a rural church in Georgia. Shortly thereafter he moved to Washington, DC, where he led a large
Presbyterian church and was later appointed twice to
serve as the United States Senate Chaplain.[24]

It may have seemed foolhardy to Marshall's family
for him to leave Scotland and come to America when
he had no immediate source of income. Without knowing the great impact he would have on this new nation,
yet unwilling to just daydream of that which might be,
he took what faltering steps he could towards realizing
his dream.

His experience taught him to say, "Small deeds
done are better than great deeds planned."[25]

Marshall's words are so insightful. In one short
sentence he reveals our propensity towards procrasti-
nation rather than action. Too often we are waiting for
that elusive "great opportunity" rather than taking the
ones that sit right in front of us, disguised as our

everyday lives. We delay pursuing the great deeds because we neglect to see the value of the small ones.

GET OFF THE TREADMILL

Another factor that pushes us towards the land of good intentions is the hectic pace of life, which keeps us running on a never-ending treadmill. Out of breath and longing for relief we pant, "Someday I'm going to get off this treadmill and do the things that really matter. I'm going to spend more time with family and friends. I'm going to live a healthier lifestyle. I'm going to take up a hobby. I'm going to take more vacation time. I'm going to improve my financial situation."

We say all these things in earnest, sincerely intending to follow through. Unfortunately, there seems to be an endless list of reasons why we can't do those things right now: "When things slow down at work," "When business picks up," "Maybe in the New Year," "When the kids are grown," "When we get out of debt," "When the economy is more stable," "When I feel better," "After they apologize to me," "Once they stop doing that, I will be able to...," "If they would just make a decision, then I could...," "Once I retire."

Just as a side note, the statistics we previously discussed show that retirement is not a good time to do the things you always dreamed of doing. According to the national average life-span, if you work till sixty-five, you only have ten years left to do it all. If our plans were impossible to accomplish in sixty-five years, what logic would tell us we could do them in ten? In addition, the latter years are typically limited by diminished physical stamina and health as well as a reduced income. Many people plan to travel in these "golden" years, but fail to realize that because of these issues, and higher costs for travel insurance, they are unable to do so.

Whenever we make a declaration of action but add a statement of limitation, we have unknowingly disempowered ourselves. When we say, "I'm going to do this, *when...*" we have declared an intended action but we have limited it by stating we are waiting for something to happen before we take action. We have transferred responsibility from ourselves to something or someone we believe must change before we can act. In effect, we have taken our future out of our hands and placed it into someone else's.

> The truth is we cannot control anything or anyone other than ourselves.

We cannot entrust our most precious pursuits to people and events beyond our influence. The truth is we cannot control anything or anyone other than ourselves. If we forfeit our future to others, we will find ourselves in a futile struggle to manipulate and control those whom we believe have power over us. We must take the responsibility to initiate change in our lives. Don't empower others to direct your life; empower yourself.

Friedrich Schiller was a German Dramatist who lived from 1759–1805. He once said, "Lose not yourself in a far off time, seize the moment that is thine."[26]

Schiller warns us not to be content with dreaming about the future but actually living in the present. In reality, all we have is the present. If we are not doing the things we value most now, we are not guaranteed an opportunity in the future. Today is the tomorrow we talked about yesterday. Our present lives are a result of yesterday's choices.

HORSEBACK RIDING

My hobby and long-time passion is horseback riding. I have often said that my therapist is my horse. There is something about being with a horse that just melts my troubles away.

For as long as I've been riding I've said, "One day I'm going to take a week-long ride through the Rocky Mountains." I've also declared, "I'm going to gallop bareback through the foaming ocean surf." And to finish the fantasy, I speak dreamily of, "Riding through a warm meadow filled with the fragrance of wildflowers and a gentle breeze flowing through my hair."

> Today is the tomorrow we talked about yesterday.

Writing this chapter has reluctantly awakened me from my happy reverie to the somewhat depressing reality that I am living in the land of good intentions. If I ever actually intend to make these fantasies a reality, a few things need to happen: I need an old trail-broke pony, not the spirited steed I currently possess; I

> **The only proof that you genuinely desire something you do not yet possess is evidenced by your tangible pursuit of it.**

actually have to pay some money to get to these exotic locations; and I have to change the kind of riding I am doing now.

If I'm really honest with myself, I am not that invested in these good intentions. If I was, I would be taking at least some steps towards them. So it is with you. The only proof that you genuinely desire something you do not yet possess is evidenced by your tangible pursuit of it.

THE TWO SONS

The Bible tells a story about a man who had two sons. One was a bit self-willed and not afraid to defy his father. The second was much more compliant and always careful to say the right thing.

> Tell me what you think of this story: A man had two sons. He went up to the first and said, "Son, go out for the day and work in the vineyard."

The son answered, "I don't want to." Later on he thought better of it and went.

The father gave the same command to the second son. He answered, "Sure, glad to." But he never went.

Which of the two sons did what the father asked? They said, "The first."[27]

These two brothers illustrate the reality of good intentions—they don't mean anything and they don't change anything unless acted upon. The second son may have had every intention of going to work that day, but something probably came up. It might have even been a *"legitimate"* excuse, but the result was still the same—he never did what he said he would do.

> **Intention without action leads to self-deception.**

Another thing this parable illustrates is the deceptive quality of good intentions. Secretly, the second son might have considered himself a better son than the first because he initially agreed to do what their father had asked. The second son may have congratulated himself by thinking, "I may not get to it today, but at least Dad will be happy, thinking I will get around to it eventually."

We, like the second son, tell ourselves that because we intend to do it, we are okay. However, intention without action leads to self-deception. In this state, we are not living in reality but in the imaginary world we have created called the land of good intentions.

It is tempting to point fingers at the second son and say what a terrible guy he was, but maybe we need to look at our own lives first. Do we allow ourselves the indulgence of good intentions but expect everyone else to produce results? When someone gives us their word, are we offended when they don't come through for us? We often judge others by their actions but judge ourselves by our intentions.

The good news is that we can all be like the first son simply by making a choice. No matter how far we are from where we want to be, no matter how much time has passed, we can take the first step towards our goal. Insanity is doing the same thing and expecting different results. We can stop the insanity and change the course of our lives simply by doing something different.

A LATE BLOOMER

A great example of someone who proved it's never too late to start something new was Harland David Sanders, better known as Colonel Sanders, who lived from September 9, 1890–December 16, 1980.

Sanders' father passed away, leaving a young Harland to cook while his mother worked to provide for the family. Hunger and necessity dictated that Harland leave formal education in the seventh grade. An unhappy relationship with his new stepfather forced him out of his home and into the army at age sixteen. He falsified his date of birth to secure a post that he served in Cuba.

After release from the army, Harland drifted in his employment from steamboat pilot, to insurance salesman, to railroad fireman and even farming. At age forty he obtained a service station in Corbin, Kentucky, where he drew from his childhood experience to prepare tasty chicken dishes for his patrons in his adjoining living quarters.

As Harland's local popularity grew, he seized the opportunity to purchase a motel and its 142-seat restaurant. There, for the next nine years he perfected his "secret recipe" for pressure-frying chicken. Not only did he corner the market on an original taste with his eleven herbs and spices, he also developed a more efficient method of cooking chicken.

Misfortune again visited Sanders at the ripe age of sixty-five. His restaurant, once located on a busy road, was now forced to close due to the new interstate highway which redirected the traffic and his customers.

> **Tomorrow is the enemy of today.**

Undaunted, Sanders devised a plan to begin selling franchise opportunities to investors. With meagre capital, he took one hundred and five dollars from his first Social Security check to embark on this new venture. Ten years later, he had turned his small investment into two million dollars, and subsequently sold his US operations to a group of Kentucky businessmen while retaining the Canadian businesses to collect franchise fees.[28]

Despite a lifetime of struggles and disappointments, this man refused to quit. He kept moving towards his dream. He was unwilling to live in the land of good intentions even when most people his age would have looked for a comfortable retirement. Colonel Sanders knew that if he stayed too long in the land of good intentions he would spend his last days in the wilderness of regret.

Sanders believed so strongly in his dream that he used his Social Security cheque to pursue it. Most senior citizens would never part with their pension for a risky investment, but the Colonel was not like most senior citizens. He refused to make excuses (including getting too old) for not reaching his goal. He poured his life and passion into each day without reservation for the next.

Remember that tomorrow is the enemy of today. Never put off till tomorrow what you can do today. Live today. Act today.

4

Comfortable Coffins

HIDE AND SEEK

MY MATERNAL GRANDMOTHER grew up in England, where her father was a circuit preacher. He would travel from village to village on horseback, sharing the good news with folks all over the English countryside. To supplement his income, he also converted part of their home into a workshop where he built coffins. My grandmother told me how she and her siblings would sneak into the workshop and play hide and seek in the empty coffins.

Great-Grandfather built coffins of every description, from simple pine boxes to ornately carved caskets. One thing they all had in common—they were soft, warm and comfortable. I am not sure if he knew the games his children were playing in the coffins. I expect he thought that the only people in his coffins were corpses.

After all, coffins are designed for the dead—not for the living. They may look more attractive than most of our furniture and softer than our own bed, but I am sure none of us would want to make our home in a coffin…or would we?

We may not take up residence in a silk-lined oak casket, but many of us have slain and buried our dreams in coffins of our own design. The desire for comfort kills the passion of the soul. This desire for comfort is why a young man gets a degree in accounting when he really wanted to go to art school. It is why the young mother chooses to run a daycare in her home rather than going back to school so she can have the career she always wanted. It is why the frustrated pastor stays at his church when his heart burns for the mission field. It is why the unhappy couple stay together long after the love has left their sterile marriage.

The fiery evangelist Reinhardt Bonnke once said his divine assignment was not so much to comfort the afflicted but to afflict the comfortable. We need to be pushed out of our coffins of comfort if we ever hope to experience terminal living.

THE TEST OF SUCCESS

An American travelling minister named Mark Hankins claims there are two tests we must pass in life. One is the test of failure. The other is of success. He believes the test of success is much harder to pass. This is because success has the tendency to make us

> **The desire for comfort kills the passion of the soul.**

forget where we came from and where we were going. In other words, success can actually destroy our original purpose and rob us of reaching our full potential.

A bright young man enters law school, dreaming of the day when he can defend the less fortunate who are without financial means to obtain quality legal counsel. However, after a few years of practice he soon discovers that paying his student loans, the mortgage on his penthouse, and the lease on his BMW require that he take on "better paying clients." Before he realizes it, the wealthy clients are demanding more and more of his time. Soon he finds it easy to justify the lack of pro-bono cases, as he says he can't help anybody if he's broke. At the end of his thirty-five years of practice, he congratulates himself on a successful career, measured by his prestige and material affluence. He only has a slight twinge of remorse for a long-forgotten dream never realized.

Being successful is not bad. However, the way we define success can be. If our definition of success is amassing material possessions, then the pursuit of things will dominate our lives, rather than the pursuit of purpose.

As ironic as it sounds, good can be the enemy of best. A little success can steal our greatest potential. Henry Ford and the Ford Motor Company are a perfect example of this principle.

HENRY FORD

In 1903, Henry Ford had already established enough credibility in the automobile industry to procure almost thirty-thousand dollars from investors, which he used to found the Ford Motor Company. He did not disappoint his investors, but began making profitable returns from the start. The introduction of the Model T in 1908 only served to skyrocket the company's initial success.

Ford proved to be unparalleled in the industry through the implementation of the assembly line principle. The assembly line reduced the price of Model T production from $850 in 1908 to $360 in 1916. This allowed the market of potential buyers to mushroom from ten thousand to well over a staggering seven hundred thousand customers during the same time period.

Though Ford began his company with other investors, by 1920 he had positioned himself as the sole owner of the world's largest industrial enterprise. His empire at its pinnacle in 1927 reported close to $700 million in undistributed earnings as well as billions more in holdings.

The early part of Ford's career was marked with incomparable creativity and foresight. However, these qualities did not follow him into his later years. He was unwilling to revise any of his original ideas on production or labour policies, despite the obviously negative repercussions his company was experiencing.

Forced only by threat of collapse, Ford agreed to introduce the Model A in favor of the Model T. However, his reticence for change afforded other automobile companies the opportunity to seize a sizeable portion of the market that Ford was never able to regain.

The brilliance Ford displayed in the automobile industry was unfortunately overshadowed by his narrow mindset towards others. His prejudice was displayed in the many anti-Semitic articles he wrote. His stubbornness was evident in his fight against unionization. His dictatorial style of leadership bore no forbearance for modern management practices.

> We must strive not for comfort but for purpose.

Because of Ford's intolerance for change, the company which once generated more wealth than any other in the American economy was splintered. By the mid-1930s, it was destitute of any clear leadership and by 1940 the company was in critical condition, losing over a million dollars a day. Before the company was utterly ruined, the family forced Ford to relinquish control to his grandson, Henry Ford II in 1945.[29]

Ford's success had not only robbed him of his full potential, but it hindered those around him. The test of success is one we will all face. We must strive not for comfort but for purpose.

When we experience a measure of success, we often get stuck in a rut like Henry Ford did with his Model T. A rut is simply a grave with both ends kicked out.[30] We become blind to new ideas and ways of doing things. We resist those who challenge us. We hold a death grip on our success which will not allow new life to flow in. We are unwilling to take new risks. A mind in this condition is unable to conceive new thoughts. A heart becomes stifled and eventually grows cold.

This is not living—it is merely existence. You were born for more than this. What would you attempt to do if you knew it was impossible to fail and money was no object? There is untapped potential in you. Dare to break out of your comfortable coffin and begin living.

Motivational speaker and author Mike Murdock says it so plainly in his book, *Dream Seeds*: "Yesterday is in the tomb. Tomorrow is in the womb. Today is really your life."[31]

5

FAIL TO PLAN—PLAN TO FAIL

MAKING A LIVING OR MAKING A LIFE

A TRIP TO your local bookstore's self-help section will reveal no shortage of information on how to plan your life. Titles like Steps to Success, Habits of Successful People, Developing a 5-Year Plan, Goal-Setting, Managing Your Finances, and Time Management are just a few that may line the shelves. While the information these books provide is useful for making a good living, they may not necessarily be useful for making a good life. The vast majority of these books simply reflect a North American culture which celebrates individualism and materialism rather than community and relationships.

> **Change is not an event, but a process we must be committed to.**

To plan a terminal life, we need more than self-help tips. We need to make a conscious choice each day to live for something greater than our own gratification. This kind of daily planning and living requires a quantum shift in our thinking. This kind of change is not an event, but a process we must be committed to. C. S. Lewis had this to say about change:

It may be hard for an egg to turn into a
would be a jolly sight harder for it to lear
while remaining an egg. We are like eggs at present. And you cannot go on indefinitely being just
an ordinary, decent egg. We must be hatched or go
bad.[32]

Nobody wants to be a rotten egg. We all want to
spread our wings and fly. However, without a definite
plan to grow and change, we are doomed to decay.

THE POWER OF HABIT

How do we devise a plan to grow? Does it require a
monumental, life-altering event, a personal life coach,
or a supreme exercise of our organizational skills? Certainly these things can help de-
velop a personal growth plan.
However, the greatest force that
moves us towards personal
growth is our daily routines or
habits. In fact, unless your plan
becomes your habit it will fail.

> The greatest
> force that
> moves us to-
> wards personal
> growth is our
> daily routines
> or habits.

Aristotle wisely understood this principle, and
said, "We are what we repeatedly do. Excellence, then,
is not an act, but a habit."[33]

In devising a personal growth plan, we need not
strive for a spectacular achievement, but small victo-
ries every day. We all know someone who decided to
lose fifty pounds so they could look good for a special

event only to put it all back on soon after. They may have changed their diet for a while, but they never changed their habits.

Many people dream of doing something significant with their lives that will really impact the world. Unfortunately, their daily routines and habits are not moving them towards anything but the couch and the television remote control. The secret to terminal living is held in our daily routines.

Renowned scientist Lloyd George Elliot illustrated well how habits form your life when he said:

> The long span of the bridge of your life is supported by countless cables called habits, attitudes, and desires. What you do in life depends upon what you are and what you want. What you get from life depends upon how much you want it. How much you are willing to work and plan and cooperate and use your resources. The long span of the bridge of your life is supported by countless cables that you are spinning now, and that is why today is such an important day. Make the cables strong![34]

LIFE HAPPENS

I got married when I was eighteen. I had never lived on my own, written a check, or applied for a loan. In short I had no real plan and was ill-prepared for life. I was content for many years to follow along with whatever life presented and whatever changes my husband's career choices imposed upon me. I was for the most part comfortable with being a wife and a mom and taking whatever part-time employment fit into our family's schedule.

However, as the years passed and the children left home, I found myself confronted with disturbing thoughts, like, "Is this what I really want to do with the rest of my life? What are my gifts, passions and dreams?" I was disquieted with the realization that I had no definitive answer to these questions.

I had failed to plan for life. I had just let life happen. Now in my forties, I finally grasped the need for me to devise a plan. I made a decision to pursue a degree in counselling. Attending the classes was relatively easy, but the homework proved to be a challenge.

In spite of also working full-time, I forced myself to devote one hour to study each day. Soon it became a habit to sit down at the computer and hammer out a few pages every evening. Slowly, as I finished the courses one by one, my confidence grew that I would actually attain my goal.

Five years later, with my doctorate degree, I can attest to the power of habits and the plan that inspires them.

SCROOGE

A character familiar to most of us whose habits were altogether selfish is Ebenezer Scrooge from Charles

Dickens' novel *A Christmas Carol.* Scrooge was the miserly, grumpy old man whose favorite expression was, "Bah, humbug!" Christmas was particularly a bad time for Scrooge, as he viewed it as an unnecessary break in his work schedule and a depletion of his precious store of money.

On Christmas Eve, as Scrooge was getting ready for bed, he had a ghostly visitation from his old business partner, Jacob Marley. Prior to his death seven years earlier, Marley, like Scrooge, had been cruel and heartless to the less fortunate. He was thus condemned to forever wander the Earth as a prisoner of his own greed. Marley delivered a grave warning to Scrooge—he would suffer the same fate if he did not respond appropriately to the three spirits that would soon visit him: Past, Present, and Future.

> **Our habits will eventually determine our destiny.**

If you remember the story, you know Scrooge realized the error of his ways after seeing a vision of his own forgotten grave and begged for another chance. When he awoke from his nightmare, he discovered he had been given an opportunity to repent after all. Scrooge delightedly amended his miserly ways to become the picture of charity.[35]

We all love this story because we would like to believe that we too could have a second chance to make things right in our lives. Unfortunately, life is not a dress rehearsal—it is a live performance. That means we have one chance to get it right. Without a plan, we will not succeed. Our habits will eventually determine our destiny.

The Bible has a story similar to Scrooge's, only it has a much different ending. It is about an unnamed rich man and a beggar named Lazarus.

THE RICH MAN AND THE BEGGAR

There was a certain rich man who was splendidly clothed in purple and fine linen and who lived each day in luxury. At his gate lay a poor man named Lazarus who was covered with sores. As Lazarus lay there longing for scraps from the rich man's table, the dogs would come and lick his open sores.

Finally, the poor man died and was carried by the angels to be with Abraham. The rich man also died and was buried, and his soul went to the place of the dead. There, in torment, he saw Abraham in the far distance with Lazarus at his side.

The rich man shouted, "Father Abraham, have some pity! Send Lazarus over here to dip the tip of his finger in water and cool my tongue. I am in anguish in these flames."

But Abraham said to him, "Son, remember that during your lifetime you had everything you wanted, and Lazarus had nothing. So now he is here being comforted, and you are in anguish. And besides, there is a great chasm separating us. No one can cross over to you from here, and no one can cross over to us from there."

Then the rich man said, "Please, Father Abraham, at least send him to my father's home.

For I have five brothers, and I want him to warn them so they don't end up in this place of torment."

But Abraham said, "Moses and the prophets have warned them. Your brothers can read what they wrote."

The rich man replied, "No, Father Abraham! But if someone is sent to them from the dead, then they will repent of their sins and turn to God."

But Abraham said, "If they won't listen to Moses and the prophets, they won't listen even if someone rises from the dead."[36]

The rich man in this story resembles Charles Dickens' character Scrooge in that he was miserly and cruel to the less fortunate. Unlike Scrooge, however, he did not wake up from a bad dream with a second chance to redeem himself.

> **Our deeds once written cannot be erased.**

He realized too late that he should have invested his life and resources more generously.

The rich man's belated concern finally shifted from himself to his family after his death. He asked for a visitation of spirits similar to what Scrooge had so that his brothers would not make the same mistake he had. This request was denied. Again we see that real life is not a Dickens novel. However, our lives are writing a story nonetheless. Our deeds once written cannot be erased.

What will be written on your epitaph? What are you doing right now that is making a positive impact in someone else's life? If you have come to the realization that your habits are leading you down the wrong path, the good news is you can adjust your life's course right now. You don't need a ghostly visitation, just a decision. You don't have to make a flow chart, PowerPoint slides or a five-year projection. You just need to change your daily routine.

Confucius once stated accurately that: "Men's natures are alike; it is their habits that separate them."[37]

Similarly, American Theologian Tryon Edwards declared, "Thoughts lead on to purpose, purpose leads on to actions, actions form habits, habits decide character and character fixes our destiny."[38]

A journey begins with the first step. Have the courage to take that step today and every day. Don't be discouraged if progress seems slow. Stick to the plan.Remember what Mark Twain once said: "Habit is habit and not to be flung out of the window by any man, but coaxed downstairs a step at a time."[39]

6

FACE YOUR FEAR

FLYING A FIGHTER plane in World War I required the ability to confront and conquer your fear. One such courageous pilot and Medal of Honor recipient was Edward Vernon Rickenbacker (1890–1973). He faced fear daily during his career, and learned that: "Courage is doing what you're afraid to do. There can be no courage unless you're scared."[40]

PERSONAL STRUGGLES

As a young girl, I was very shy and insecure. I hated my overweight body, my pimply face and the second-hand clothes I wore. Finally passing through puberty, I lost weight, got rid of my acne and landed a job so I could buy my own clothes. On the outside I portrayed a confident, intelligent, and attractive young woman. However, deep within my soul the fear remained hidden and continued to dominate my life.

As a result of this lack of confidence, I avoided intimacy with people, excused myself from any public engagements, and was suspicious and critical of others. I was desperate to insulate myself from the pain of rejection.

It took many years of struggle before I finally realized it was impossible to avoid pain in life. It's said that pain is inevitable, but suffering is optional. I finally learned that the only way to conquer my fear was to face it head on. My life began to change as I finally let go and allowed the walls I had built around me to crumble.

> "He who is not everyday conquering some fear has not learned the secret of life."

My life's work has always been involved in helping people, hence there have been countless opportunities for me to retreat behind my walls of fear. However, the best defence has proven to be a good offense. I regularly shake hands with people I don't know, speak in front of people, and provide counsel to the hurting. Is it easy? Not in the slightest! I still have to muster my courage every time I do it. But I refuse to be held back by my fear any longer.

Fear paralyzes you. Faith frees you. Fear shrinks your world. Faith enlarges it. Ralph Waldo Emerson said, "He who is not everyday conquering some fear has not learned the secret of life."[41]

Nelson Mandella was imprisoned twenty-seven years for trying to bring freedom to his people. He had this to say about facing fear:

> Our deepest fear is not that we are inadequate. Our deepest fear is that we are powerful beyond measure. It is our light, not our darkness that most frightens us. We ask ourselves, who am I to be brilliant, gorgeous, talented and fabulous? Actually,

who are you not to be? You are a child of God. Your playing small doesn't serve the world. There is nothing enlightened about shrinking so that other people won't feel insecure around you. We were born to make manifest the glory of God that is within us. It is not just in some of us: it's in every-one. And when we let our own light shine, we un-consciously give other people permission to do the same. As we are liberated from our own fear, our presence automatically liberates others.[42]

KING GEORGE VI

In the latter part of 2010, *The King's Speech*, was re-leased and became a box office smash, winning four Oscars. The film was based on the true story of the life of King George VI, whose greatest fear was public speaking due to his severe speech impediment. When his father, King George V, died in the winter of 1936, his brother David became king. However it was a short-lived reign as he abdicated the throne and Bertie (the family name for King George VI) was compelled to take on a role that would force him to face his worst fear—public speaking.

Through his great courage and the help of a whimsical and unorthodox therapist named Lionel Logue, he conquered his fear to inspire Britain and all of Europe in their defiance of Hitler's Nazi war machine.[43]

FEAR CONQUERED

A few years ago, my husband and I embarked on a venture that had the potential to finish us both in our personal lives and in our careers. We agreed to take over an institution that was in serious debt, the morale of the staff was at an all-time low, regional support had disintegrated, and the facility itself had fallen into such ill repair that it was under threat of closure by the local health authorities.

Needless to say, we were both under an inordinate amount of job stress, which filtered into our personal lives. There were many days we wanted to pack up and run but something within us kept saying, "If you leave now you'll never know what might have been."

Slowly, things began to turn. Employee productivity increased with staffing changes; regional support grew as our corporate reputation improved; as cash flow increased, we were able to renovate and bring the facility to a standard of excellence. Today the institution is flourishing.

There were many days we wondered how we could keep going. The emotion of fear and failure haunted us on every side. Yet we believed that if we just did what we knew to do, the resources, the favor and the people would come. It was simple faith that conquered our fear.

The poet, playwright, and author Patrick Overton said that simple faith is the key to overcoming fear:

When you have come to the edge of all the light that you know and are about to drop off into the darkness of the unknown, faith is knowing one of two things will happen: There will be something solid to stand on or you will be taught to fly.[44]

It's time to take that step of faith into the unknown. You will never know the thrill of flying till you're willing to leave the security of the nest. You will never walk on water till you step out of the boat. Refuse to let fear rob you of the amazing terminal life you were destined to live.

7

NO RISK—NO REWARD

HOCKEY LEGEND WAYNE Gretzky once said, "You'll always miss 100% of the shots you don't take."[45] His simple statement illustrates the need to risk failure in order to achieve success. Without taking a risk you will never receive the reward.

COWBOY COUNTRY

We were just getting established as a young married couple in the early 80s. My husband had a good job, we had just purchased our first home and our oldest child was born. Things were comfortable and progressing in the typical suburban fashion.

At this time, we received a call from a good friend who had just become the director of a large youth and children's ranch in the heart of "cowboy country" in Western Canada. He phoned to ask if we would be willing to help him and his wife run the camp for the whopping salary of six hundred dollars a month. Whether it was merely youthful naivety or divine direction, we were thrilled at the opportunity to positively impact the lives of thousands of young people.

Our family, though they were gracious, thought we were crazy to leave the security and comfort of our life in the city. How would we ever afford to buy another house, a new car, or send our kids to university making six hundred dollars a month?

The years we spent at the ranch were lean financially but rich in every other way. We saw countless young people's lives transformed through the work we were privileged to be a part of. Our time there laid a foundation for terminal living which we have carried to this day.

As an epilogue to this story, all the material things that we "risked" to take the position at the ranch have been returned to us in abundance. We have discovered that *whatever you give away for the sake of love always comes back to you.*

PENNY CHENERY TWEEDY

Someone who understood and embraced the value of taking a risk was Penny Chenery Tweedy. She was a housewife and mother who owned the famous American Thoroughbred racehorse, Secretariat. She agreed to take over her ailing father's stable, regardless of her lack of horseracing savvy. Shortly thereafter, Penny's father suffered a stroke and died, leaving Penny and her brother Hollis to inherit the indebted estate. Despite the fact that Penny

> **Whatever you give away for the sake of love always comes back to you.**

needed six million dollars to pay estate taxes, she refused to sell Secretariat, whose stable name was Red.

Instead, Penny came up with a plan to syndicate Red, and sold thirty-two shares worth more than six million dollars. These shares were contingent on Red winning a three-year-old distance race. When she tried to sell a share to a rival named Ogden Phipps, he offered to buy Red for eight million dollars. Penny declined his proposal. That year

> "Behold the turtle. He makes progress only when he sticks his neck out."

was 1973 and against all odds, Secretariat went on to become the first Triple Crown winner in twenty-five years and one of the greatest racehorses of all time, still holding two unbroken records today.[46]

Penny had to be willing to risk losing her reputation and her family's fortune to reach her goal. She gave up the comfort of her home and family, endured great criticism from friend and foe alike, suffered numerous setbacks, and above all she fought the demons of self-doubt. She was tempted to head back to the bench more than once but she stayed on the ice, she kept skating, she took the shot and to everyone's surprise, she scored.

Everyone admires and wants to be the one who scores. We all love to feel the thrill of victory and the excitement of being on the cutting edge. But are we ready to risk it all to gain the reward? James Bryant Conant sagely advised those who would pursue their dreams: "Behold the turtle. He makes progress only when he sticks his neck out."[47]

Many people complain about their boring jobs, lack of friends, and chronic fatigue. Void of any enthusiasm, they drag themselves out of bed and shuffle through their lacklustre days. If you were to ask these same people if they would like a more fulfilling and exciting life, most of them would say, *"Yes!"* until they realize they would be required to stick their neck out— take a risk. The fact is that without risk there is no reward.

SEAN LITTON

Sean Litton proved he was not afraid to take a risk. Sean was a brilliant lawyer with a successful career at an elite national law firm. He was challenged by an opportunity presented to him to leave his prestigious position and relocate his family to the Philippines and use his legal expertise to help free young girls trapped in the sex trade. His reaction was recorded in Gary Haugen's book, *Just Courage*:

> I was not so afraid of going as I was of coming back. I was at the top of my profession; I could do anything I wanted. If I went overseas for three or four years to work for some little Christian group, I was sure I would come back to a crappy job, work with crappy people, live in a crappy house, and wear crappy slacks as I drink my crappy coffee while driving my crappy car.

But I just thought, if I can rescue one child from the unspeakable horror of forced prostitution, it would outweigh any sacrifice I could possibly make. How could any sacrifice I make, how could it possibly compare to the daily abuse and suffering of a child locked in a brothel forced to serve four to seven customers a day?[48]

Sean accepted the challenge, took the risk and established an office in the Philippines, then one in Thailand, and eventually directed efforts in the entire region of Southeast Asia. Through the years he has seen hundreds of lives transformed because he was willing to take a risk. He valued the impact he was making in these children's lives of greater reward than his former six-figure income.

We don't need to train a racehorse or move to Asia to take a risk. Sometimes the biggest risks are those closest to us. When our hearts are broken, sometimes the biggest risk is simply offering our heart to another person. When our trust is betrayed, the scariest thing can be to trust again. Whatever you are facing, remember: "To love is to risk not being loved in return. To hope is to risk pain. To try is to risk failure, but risk must be taken because the greatest hazard in life is to risk nothing."[49]

President Theodore Roosevelt once said, "Far better is it to dare mighty things, to win glorious triumphs, even though chequered by failure... than to rank with those poor spirits who neither enjoy nor suffer much, because they live in a gray twilight that knows not victory nor defeat."[50]

PAUL BRANDT

Award-winning Canadian country music artist Paul Brandt wrote a song called *Risk*, which captures the essence of its title. The lyrics describe someone who dared to take chances rather than play it safe—learning and laughing at mistakes, and living with a sense of wonder and adventure. A portion of the chorus illustrates how Paul understands that life is for living—not preserving:

> I'd rather live my whole life with a sense of aban-
> don, Squeeze every drop out, no matter what hap-
> pens. And not wonder what I missed I'd rather
> Risk.[51]

One of the most common regrets of the elderly is that they never took the risks necessary in their prime

> **Too many peo-
> ple choose to
> live with re-
> grets rather
> than conquer
> their fear.**

to experience life on a higher level. I once heard the story of a woman who always wanted to live in a warmer climate but never did simply because she was afraid to move without the guar-antee of a job. Logic would dictate that one will likely never get a job in a new location till you first take the risk to move there. Too many people choose to live with regrets rather than conquer their fear.

Living with a sense of abandon, letting life's storms carry you away, jumping off a cliff and building your wings on the way down—this is taking a risk. This is where the rewards are. This is living. The exciting life you always wanted is calling...will you answer?

8

LEAVING A LEGACY

WHILE IT IS wonderful to live an exciting, fulfilling life personally, if we fail to impact the next generation, we will have missed the most critical component of terminal living. There can be no success without a successor.

> **There can be no success without a successor.**

Leadership guru Stephen R. Covey explains:

> There are certain things that are fundamental to human fulfillment. The essence of these needs is captured in the phrase "to live, to love, to learn, to leave a legacy." The need to live is our physical need for such things as food, clothing, shelter, economical well-being, health. The need to love is our social need to relate to other people, to belong, to love and to be loved. The need to learn is our mental need to develop and to grow. And the need to leave a legacy is our spiritual need to have a sense of meaning, purpose, personal congruence, and contribution.[52]

Pacific Salmon

Perhaps one of the most vivid pictures of leaving a legacy can be found in nature with the migration of the Pacific salmon.

The upriver salmon migration is one of nature's most exciting dramas. But to the Pacific salmon... it is a long, strenuous, desperate race against time, with every obstacle taking its toll.

Pacific salmon hatch and live the first part of their lives in fresh water, then migrate to the ocean to spend their adult lives. When they reach sexual maturity, they return to the freshwater stream of their origin to lay their eggs. They make the round trip only once.

Salmon spawn in virtually all types of freshwater habitat, from intertidal areas to high mountain streams. Pacific salmon may swim hundreds, even thousands, of miles to get back to the stream where they hatched. However, only a small percentage of salmon live to reach their natal stream or spawning grounds. Those males that survive the trip are often gaunt, with grotesquely humped backs, hooked jaws, and battle-torn fins. The females are swollen with a pound or more of eggs. Both have large white patches of bruised skin on their backs and sides.

Since salmon do not feed once they leave the ocean, some will die on the way because they lack enough stored body fat to make the trip. Many will be caught in fishermen's nets. Those that evade the nets may have to swim through polluted waters near cities. Many must make their way over power dams, leaping up from one tiny pool to the next along cement stair- step cascades called fish ladders. In the tributary streams, waterfalls and rapids are steep and swift enough to eliminate all but the strongest. Otters, eagles, and bears stalk the salmon in shallow riffles. Once on the spawning grounds, the fish battle each other: females against females for places to nest; males against males for available females.

The female builds her nest, called a redd, by agitating the bottom gravel with her fins and tail, and bending her body into a U shape first one way, then the other. As soon as she has excavated a depression, she settles onto it and deposits her first batch of eggs, or roe. The male then moves alongside and deposits his sperm, called milt, over the roe. The female rakes her tail back and forth to cover the redd with loose gravel. She then excavates her next redd a short distance upstream.

The process continues until all the roe and milt have been deposited. One pair of salmon may have as many as seven redds, with four or five being the average. The salmon die within a few days of spawning.[53]

We can learn a lot about terminal living from the salmon.

ADAPTABILITY

The salmon are born into one environment (fresh water), yet are required to adapt to a completely different environment (salt water) if they are to mature and complete their life cycle. The food supply, the currents, and the composition of the water itself are all completely different. If they fail to adapt they will eventually die never having reached their potential.

Like the salmon, we will not be able to mature if we stay in our current environment. Our growth requires change. The relationships, ac-

> **Our growth requires change.**

tivities, knowledge, skills, and moral standards of our current environment will not be sufficient for what lies ahead. Our present place of self-sufficiency and comfort cannot be our permanent residence. If we stay where we are we will stagnate and eventually die never realizing our full potential.

Turn of the century French writer and winner of the Nobel Prize for literature, Anatole France[54,] said, "All changes, even the most longed for, have their melancholy; for what we leave behind us is a part of ourselves; we must die to one life before we can enter another."[55]

TIMING

There is an internal mechanism within this remarkable fish that triggers an outward response. The salmon instinctively know when it is time for them to move. They have used their preparatory time of growth wisely by feeding regularly, and now they perceive they are ready for their heroic journey.

Something within them signals it's time to quit attending to their own needs and to focus all their energy towards attending to the needs of the next generation.

There are seasons in all our lives. In our early years, like the salmon, we are consumed with feeding and growing ourselves.

This is a necessary, preparatory stage without which we would lack the means to invest in the next generation. As we mature, however, there is an instinctive need to reproduce. Personal success begins to lose its lustre as we recognize our need to help others succeed.

The Governor of Washington, Christine Gregoire, aptly declared: "It is up to us to live up to the legacy that was left for us, and to leave a legacy that is worthy of our children and of future generations."[56]

DIRECTION

Without any external guidance, these extraordinary fish know precisely the location they need to get to. Their destiny is invisibly yet undeniably imprinted within them. While living in the ocean, they would have mingled with fish from many different spawning grounds. If we use our imaginations, we can envision a salmon might be pulled in many directions by the relationships he forms with the other salmon. Without an internal sense of direction, he might be tempted to simply follow the rest of the fish. Yet his inner GPS is fixed and compels him to swim to a predetermined location.

Each one of us has a predetermined, invisible, undeniable destiny. It is universal yet unique to each person. It is universal in that each of us has the need to leave our footprint on the sands of history—no one wants to be forgotten. It is unique in that each of our footprints is distinctive and each of our contributions to the next generation will be different. We are compelled to follow our own personal GPS to a specific place, to a particular group of people. We are not called to impact everyone, but we are called to impact someone.

American poet E.E. Cummings broke new literary ground with his unique writing style. His work inspired a whole new generation. He once said, "To be nobody but yourself in a world which is doing its best, night and day, to make you everybody else means to fight the hardest battle which any human being can fight; and never stop fighting."[57]

DETERMINATION

Millions of salmon embark on the great migration to their spawning grounds. Very few complete the perilous journey. However, the fish don't let their fellow travelers' lack of success keep them from their own. They refuse to allow obstacles like swimming hundreds of miles upstream or jumping over waterfalls to deter them. Nor do they allow the teeth of a bear or the claws of an eagle to paralyze them with fear. They don't let the length of the journey discourage them.

They accept that life is a struggle and are committed to fight for the right to procreate.

Many people embark on their journeys with great passion, but allow life's struggles to make them give up the fight before reaching their destination. We can't expect to float lazily downstream and enjoy the same rewards as those who spent their entire lives fighting for every mile they swam upstream. There will be many enemies along the banks, treacherous waterfalls, and a lot of long lonely days on route to our destinations. When we accept adversity we will be able to conquer it.

> When we accept adversity we will be able to conquer it.

The great American baseball player and coach Tommy Lasorda once stated: "The difference between the impossible and the possible lies in a man's determination."[58] Sir Winston Churchill lived his life with a passion that inspired all those he met. He had this to say on the importance of determination: "Success is not final, failure is not fatal: it is the courage to continue that counts."[59]

SACRIFICE

In their prime, adult Pacific salmon have great lives as they enjoy the comfort and abundance of the ocean. It is only out of an all-consuming need to breed that they forfeit this delightful existence. They subject themselves to wounding, fatigue, depravation, and even death. All is invested in the next generation. Their brief life has purpose because they are willing to sacrifice it for those who will follow after their same pattern.

Just as a seed must be buried and die in the soil before a new plant can grow out of it, so it is with our lives. Sacrifice is the seed we must plant for others. Our lives, represented in our time, our wisdom, our love, and our resources, once planted will leave a legacy for the next generation.

A woman who understood sacrifice was Maria W. Chapman. She lived during the period of the American abolition, and worked closely with William Lloyd Garrison.[60] Maria bravely withstood violent opposition as she fought for the emancipation of those trapped in slavery. She knew that her sacrifice would ensure the freedom of not only the people of her day but for all who were yet to be born. She defied tradition and prejudice and disregarded personal safety while she courageously proclaimed these words that continue to echo through history: "Grudge no expense—yield to no opposition—forget fatigue—till, by the strength of prayer and sacrifice, the spirit of love shall have overcome."[61]

> **Sacrifice is the seed we must plant for others.**

EXTINCTION

Somehow these amazing marine creatures know that if they fail to leave a legacy, it is not simply a personal loss but a loss for their entire kind. Inherently they understand that if they do not procreate, they will become extinct. Nature has a cruel but effective method of ensuring survival through a process of selection—only the strongest survive to propagate the species.

Unlike the salmon, we sometimes lose sight of the obvious certainty that if we don't leave a legacy for the next generation we will become extinct. History is full of cultures that were lost, languages forgotten, and customs assimilated all because not enough people fought to leave a legacy.

Unless we fight for the privilege of propagation, our lives and their impact will end when our heart stops beating. We each carry a unique treasure that must be handed down lest it perish with us. The tragic fact is that only a strong few grasp this truth and actually pass their treasures to the next generation. We must choose to be one of the few who live not for themselves alone but for those who will follow.

> **We each carry a unique treasure that must be handed down lest it perish with us.**

British Theologian and author Paul Scanlon shared his remarkable insight on leaving a legacy in his book, *Crossing Over*:

> What God gives us to be spent on the earth must stay on the earth. We can't take it with us; heaven doesn't need it, and God doesn't want it back. We must die empty, fully spent, with nothing held back, nothing in reserve, nothing we wish we had

done, and no one we wish we had helped. We are supposed to start full and finish empty... I refuse to die with the secret recipe, with things I didn't pass on because I enjoyed having them to myself. I refuse to die alone without spiritual sons and daughters into whom my life has been poured and who will continue to live. I refuse to die grasping a baton that I should have passed years ago.[62]

Let's not let our lives pass before we pass them to the next generation.

9

THE ULTIMATE TERMINAL LIFE

THE MAN WHO STANDS ALONE IN HISTORY

A BOOK ON terminal living would be incomplete without highlighting the man who lived the ultimate terminal life. This man lived his whole life in view of his imminent death. Every day was filled with a sense of destiny. Every conversation he had, every person he touched, every word he spoke were all done with a sense of urgent and compassionate purpose.

There has never been a man like him whose life and death so dramatically changed the world. Time and history are recorded in relation to his birth and death. His biography has sold more copies than any other book ever written.

This man never built a global corporation, but his holdings are incalculable. He never founded a political party, but his followers cover the globe. He lived only thirty-three years on this earth, but he still lives today in the hearts and lives of all who know him.

This singularly extraordinary man was Jesus of Nazareth.

I don't know where you're at in your spiritual journey, but I hope you will be open enough to consider the facts. Far beyond any person in recorded history,

Jesus demonstrated all the qualities of a terminal life as we've discussed.

1. Time is Ticking

He lived only thirty-three years (less than half the average life expectancy of his time) and yet accomplished more than anyone who could live a hundred lifetimes. Knowing his time was short did not paralyze him; it motivated him. He refused to be drawn into activities that stole his time, choosing rather to invest it into something that would last—people. In three-and-a-half brief years, he successfully trained twelve men who subsequently carried his life and teachings to the entire known world.

2. Forgotten Dreams

Jesus had one dream that he carried in his heart since he was a child. It was recorded that as early as twelve years old, he was already vocalizing his dream to *"be about [his] Father's business."*[63] What this dream entailed was revealed more fully on the day he began his public ministry at age thirty. His dream was to bring good news to the poor—to proclaim that captives would be released, the blind would see, and the oppressed would be set free, and to demonstrate that the time of the Lord's favor had come. As he drew his last breath, he declared the dream was fulfilled when he gasped, "It is finished."[64]

3.   Land of Good Intentions

Because Jesus grasped the brevity of life, he lived with a sense of urgency. He refused to procrastinate. He lived in the present and even referred to himself as the *"I am,"*[65] denoting his existence in the eternal today. He was not satisfied or deceived through good intentions. He did not rest till the job was done, often working through the night and rising before the dawn.

So committed was Jesus to keeping his promises that he stated heaven and earth would pass away before one word he said would be left undone. He never waited for others to act before he did. He showed he understood that his destiny lay in his hands, not in the hands of those around him, when he declared, *"No one takes my life from me. I give it up willingly! I have the power to give it up and the power to receive it back again, just as my Father commanded me to do."*[66]

4.   Comfortable Coffins

The desire for comfort never killed the passion of Jesus' soul. He was the oldest son of a typical Jewish family. He would have been expected to take over the family business and had indeed spent many years apprenticing with his father to do just that. He could have had a comfortable life as a carpenter, married a wife and had children. Instead he bore the reproach of his family and community to pursue the dream that burned like a fire in his bosom.

It wasn't long before everyone had heard of Jesus and great crowds met him everywhere he went. As he rode into Jerusalem, the crowds hailed him and desired to make him their King. However, he didn't allow success to blind or detour him from his higher purpose. He passed the test of success.

Jesus also faced the test of failure. The same crowd who cheered him became the one who screamed, *"Crucify him!"*[67] Everyone he had poured his life into deserted him, and one of his closest friends betrayed him to those who would kill him. Utterly alone, the flame of his passion burned unwaveringly till it was swallowed in death.

5.   Fail to Plan—Plan to Fail

Jesus never bought into the individualist self-help mindset. He was focussed and determined to live for a greater purpose than himself. He said that which brought him fulfillment was not doing whatever he wanted, but finishing the plan he received from his Father.

Jesus lived daily with his plan in view. To fulfill the plan he was deliberate about personal growth. Though not formally educated, as a young boy he amazed scholars with his self-acquired knowledge. Those who attempted to ensnare him in verbal debate were invariably confounded by his wisdom. The crowds he addressed said they had never heard anyone speak or carry themselves with such authority.

Jesus' birth, life, and even death all brought fulfillment to a divine plan of which he was a willing participant.

6.   Face Your Fear

Though he was divine, Jesus became a man who felt all the same emotions we do. Just before his crucifixion, he faced his greatest fear in a garden called Gethsemane. While he agonized in anticipation of the pain, shame, and rejection he knew he was to endure, he pleaded for his Father to make another way for the plan to be fulfilled. Yet even in that dark hour, he understood there was no other way. In steely determination, he conquered his fear, went to the cross, and embraced his sacrificial death.

7.   No Risk No Reward

Jesus put everything on the line for the dream he held in his heart. His death would be the bridge that an estranged mankind could cross to be reunited with the Father. But he had no guarantee that anyone would respond favorably to his supreme sacrifice.

Jesus endured a lifetime of ridicule from those who saw no value in what he was trying to accomplish. His own family mocked him, his enemies publicly tried to discredit him, his friends often misunderstood him, and in the end they all abandoned him.

He knew the risk he was taking, but looked optimistically towards the future and bravely declared:

Unless a grain of wheat is buried in the ground, dead to the world, it is never any more than a grain of wheat. But if it is buried, it sprouts and reproduces itself many times over. In the same way, anyone who holds on to life just as it is destroys that life. But if you let it go, reckless in your love, you'll have it forever, real and eternal.[68]

8.   Leaving a Legacy

The most extraordinary difference between Jesus and any other person who has ever left a legacy is this: every other individual has only left an example to follow. Jesus did much more—he left himself. He promised he would not just show us what to do, but that he would actually come to live inside us and empower us to do what he did. No other human being could ever offer such a wondrous legacy.

> **Jesus recognized that we needed more than an example; we needed help.**

Jesus recognized that we needed more than an example; we needed help—divine help. Before his death, he told his bewildered followers that he was going away but that he would not leave them alone. He promised he would not only return to be with them but actually reside within them and make them "come alive" in a way they never had before:

I will not leave you orphaned. I'm coming back. In just a little while the world will no longer see me, but you're going to see me because I am alive and you're about to come alive. At that moment you will know absolutely that I'm in my Father, and you're in me, and I'm in you.[69]

According to the dictionary, a legacy is:

1. A gift of property, especially personal property, as money, by will; a bequest

2. Anything handed down from the past, as from an ancestor or predecessor[70]

A legacy is by necessity a dead thing, passed down from a dead person. However, Jesus passed down a living legacy from a living person—his very life. No one else could do such a preposterous thing, but then no one else's grave is empty. Jesus is the only one who died, was raised to life, and will never die again. Jesus is the only person who could be the executor of his own will to ensure his legacy would live on.

> **Jesus is the only person who could be the executor of his own will to ensure his legacy would live on.**

Jesus didn't leave us money, property, or an inspiring biography. He left us something infinitely more valuable—himself.

10

TAKE UP THE CHALLENGE

TO LIVE A terminal life will be the greatest challenge you will ever undertake. Your resolve to live with a sense of urgency will be dulled by the deception that you have the luxury of time to pursue your passions. Your decision to live for a higher purpose will be threatened as the desire for comfort seeks to snuff it out. Your dream may at times feel like a nightmare. Your fears may sometimes overcome you. You may wonder if the reward is actually worth the risk. Regrets from past failures and disappointments may temporarily paralyze you.

Just as in a race, we will often stumble and fall short of our initial goals. But like marathon runners, we must pick ourselves up and keep going. You cannot run forward and look backwards at the same time. You may have failed yesterday, but today is a new day.

Never lose sight of the finish line that is drawing ever nearer. Life is too brief for every one of us, but just imagine if you knew you only had six weeks to live. Would you live differently than you are now? I suspect there would be a lot of things on your bucket list, a lot of people you would make amends with, and

> **You cannot run forward and look backwards at the same time.**

many loved ones you would spend more time with. Why not live today with that kind of urgency, intensity, love, and passion?

We would do well to adopt Terry Fox's attitude and the passionate promise he made to himself as he ran his last courageous race: "I will rise up to meet this new challenge face to face and prove myself worthy of life, something too many people take for granted."[71]

We cannot afford to take life for granted. It is a precious gift entrusted to us. The purpose of this treasure is not to guard it carefully in a safe, dark vault, but to bring it out into the precarious light of life and spend it all with complete abandon.

Terminal living is choosing to live life fully, purposefully, bravely, and unreservedly knowing that time is short. It is letting go of the past to reach for what lies ahead. It is living not for ourselves but for those who will follow us.

The world is crying out for men and women who are willing to live a terminal life—everyday heroes who are brave enough to face their fear, take a risk, and live sacrificially. US Senator and Governor Gaylord Nelson said, "The ultimate test of man's conscience may be his willingness to sacrifice something today for future generations whose words of thanks will not be heard."[72]

You cannot calculate the impact of your contribution into the lives of others any more than you can calculate how far the ripples will extend from a tiny pebble tossed in the ocean. Are you one of the everyday heroes willing to look beyond your own desires and hear the cries of the world around you? Can you see past yourself to those who may never be able to repay you or even offer thanks for your sacrifice?

Living a terminal life doesn't require that you be a celebrity, a political leader or anyone people might call "special." You don't have to run a cross-country marathon like Terry Fox, but you can walk across the street to a lonely widow's house. You may never inspire a nation like Winston Churchill, but you can inspire hope in the heart of a friend who just lost their job. Conquering your fear may not bring courage to a kingdom facing war like King George VI, but it may bring courage to a co-worker facing a divorce.

> **"The greatest use of life is to spend it for something that will outlast it."**

There are opportunities all around us to live terminally. What will you choose to do with your life? Will you be content to idly dream or will you dare to act? Will you remain locked in a prison of bitterness and regret, or will you break free to a life of purpose and fulfillment? Will you invest your life into future generations or squander it on temporary personal gratification? The choice is up to you. William James said truly, "The greatest use of life is to spend it for something that will outlast it."[73]

I dare you to take up the challenge and live a terminal life.

EPILOGUE: GETTING STARTED

After reading this book, you may be sitting there thinking, "I am ready to start living terminally, but exactly how do I get started?"

The only thing you need to get started is a partner. True terminal living cannot be done alone. You need someone who is experienced to help you and mentor you.

We can learn a lesson from the ox. When a young ox reaches maturity around age three, his training begins. The way the trainer teaches the young ox is by pairing him with an older, stronger, and more experienced ox. They are paired by the use of a yoke, which is typically a wooden beam fitted over the neck and shoulders and attached to the cart or load they are assigned to carry. The yoke effectively keeps the young ox in pace with his partner, yet allows the older animal to bear the bulk of the burden.

Jesus, who lived the ultimate terminal life, invites you to yoke up with him. He wants to be your partner in terminal living. Jesus said:

> If you are tired from carrying heavy burdens, come to me and I will give you rest. Take the yoke I give you. Put it on your shoulders and learn from me. I

am gentle and humble, and you will find rest. This yoke is easy to bear, and this burden is light. [74]

You may have thought that "yoking up" with Jesus would be a heavy burden, but that couldn't be farther from the truth. He's going to be the one pulling the bulk of the load. He wants to help you, not harm you. He is gentle and humble, not demanding or harsh. He wants to make your burden lighter.

All you have to do is say *"Yes"* to his invitation. In your own simple words, tell him you're tired of carrying the load alone and you want his help. Tell him you want to experience what it means to really live. He is just waiting for you to ask. He told us, *"I came so that everyone would have life, and have it in its fullest."* [75]

Life in its fullest. That is the best description anyone could have of living a terminal life. That is the gift Jesus is offering you today. My earnest prayer is that you will receive it.

ENDNOTES

[1] Terry Fox. (1979, October). Terry's letter. The Terry Fox Foundation. Retrieved May 1, 2011, from
http://www.terryfox.org/Foundation/Terrys_Letter.html

[2] Sandra Martin. (2011, June 18). Her son's legacy was kept alive and pure. The Globe and Mail. Retrieved May 2, 2011, from
http://v1.theglobeandmail.com/servlet/story/LAC.20110618.OBBET TYFOXATL/BDAStory/BDA/deaths/?pageRequested=3

[3] CBC News. (2008, January 14). Life expectancy hits 80.4 years: Statistics Canada. Retrieved May 9, 2011, from
http://www.cbc.ca/news/canada/story/2008/01/14/death-stats.html

[4] The Economist. (2007, July 19). Couch potatoes. Retrieved May 11, 2011, from
http://www.economist.com/research/articlesBySubject/displaystory.cfm?subjectid=7933596&story_id=9527126

[5] nielsenwire. (2010, February 16). Facebook users average 7 hrs a month in January as digital universe expands. Retrieved May 12, 2011, from
http://blog.nielsen.com/nielsenwire/online_mobile/facebook-users-average-7-hrs-a-month-in-january-as-digital-universe-expands/

[6] Seneca. (Mid-1st Century AD). Thinkexist.com. Retrieved May 13, 2011, from

http://thinkexist.com/quotation/we_all_sorely_complain_of_the_sho rtness_of_time/297599.html

[7] Psalm 90:12 New Living Translation **(NLT)** Holy Bible. New Living Translation copyright© 1996, 2004, 2007 by Tyndale House Foundation. Used by permission of Tyndale House Publishers Inc. Carol Stream, Illinois 60188

[8] Ecclesiastes 3:11 Amplified Bible **(AMP)** Copyright © 1954, 1958, 1962, 1964, 1965, 1987 by The Lockman Foundation

[9] Psalm103:15–16 New King James Version **(NKJV)** Copyright © 1982 by Thomas Nelson, Inc.

[10] Carl Sandburg. (n.d.). BrainyQuote.com. Retrieved May 15, 2011, from BrainyQuote.com Web site: http://www.brainyquote.com/quotes/quotes/c/carlsandbu121791.html

[11] Michael LeBoeuf. (n.d.). BrainyQuote.com. Retrieved May 15, 2011, from BrainyQuote.com Web site: http://www.brainyquote.com/quotes/quotes/m/michaelleb104467.html

[12] Francis Bacon. (n.d.). BrainyQuote.com. Retrieved May 9, 2011, from BrainyQuote.com Web site: http://www.brainyquote.com/quotes/quotes/f/francisbac106024.html

[13] Michelangelo. (n.d.). BrainyQuote.com. Retrieved May 3, 2011, from BrainyQuote.com Web site: http://www.brainyquote.com/quotes/quotes/m/michelange161309.html

[14] Genesis 37:18–20 New Living Translation **(NLT)** Holy Bible. New Living Translation copyright© 1996, 2004, 2007 by Tyndale House Foundation. Used by permission of Tyndale House Publishers Inc. Carol Stream, Illinois 60188

[15] John Barrymore. (n.d.). BrainyQuote.com. Retrieved May 18, 2011, from BrainyQuote.com Web site: http://www.brainyquote.com/quotes/quotes/j/johnbarrym161562.html

[16] Gen. 45:4–5, 7–8 Contemporary English Version **(CEV)** Copyright © 1995 by American Bible Society

[17] Randy Pausch. (2011, October 6). In Wikipedia, The Free Encyclopedia. Retrieved May 2, 2011, from http://en.wikipedia.org/w/index.php?title=Randy_Pausch&oldid=454181381

[18] Randy Pausch. (2011, October 6). In Wikipedia, The Free Encyclopedia. Retrieved May 2, 2011, from http://en.wikipedia.org/w/index.php?title=Randy_Pausch&oldid=454181381

[19] Randy Pausch. (2007, September 18). Really achieving your childhood dreams. Retrieved May 2, 2011, from http://www.cs.cmu.edu/~pausch/Randy/pauschlastlecturetranscript.pdf

[20] Randy Pausch. (2007, September 18). Really achieving your childhood dreams. Retrieved May 2, 2011, from http://www.cs.cmu.edu/~pausch/Randy/pauschlastlecturetranscript.pdf

[21] Theodore Roosevelt. (2011, November 6). In Wikipedia, The Free Encyclopedia. Retrieved May 15, 2011, from http://en.wikipedia.org/w/index.php?title=Theodore_Roosevelt&oldid=459329435

[22] Theodore Roosevelt. (n.d.). BrainyQuote.com. Retrieved May 17, 2011, from BrainyQuote.com Web site: http://www.brainyquote.com/quotes/quotes/t/theodorero109913.html

Terminal Living

[23] Thomas A. Edison. (n.d.). BrainyQuote.com. Retrieved May 15, 2011, from BrainyQuote.com Web site: http://www.brainyquote.com/quotes/quotes/t/thomasaed104931.html

[24] Peter Marshall (preacher). (2011, September 9). In Wikipedia, The Free Encyclopedia. Retrieved May 23, 2011, from http://en.wikipedia.org/w/index.php?title=Peter_Marshall_(preacher)&oldid=449261555

[25] Peter Marshall. (n.d.). BrainyQuote.com. Retrieved May 23, 2011, from BrainyQuote.com Web site: http://www.brainyquote.com/quotes/quotes/p/petermarsh104946.html

[26] Friedrich Schiller. (n.d.). BrainyQuote.com. Retrieved May 20, 2011, from BrainyQuote.com Web site: http://www.brainyquote.com/quotes/quotes/f/friedrichs154945.html

[27] Matthew 21:28–31a The Message **(MSG)** Copyright © 1993, 1994, 1995, 1996, 2000, 2001, 2002 by Eugene H. Peterson

[28] Colonel Sanders. (2011, November 15). In Wikipedia, The Free Encyclopedia. Retrieved May 19, 2011, from http://en.wikipedia.org/w/index.php?title=Colonel_Sanders&oldid=460831758

[29] John Steele Gordon. (n.d.). Answers.com. Houghton Mifflin companion to US history: Ford, Henry. Retrieved May 21, 2011, from http://www.answers.com/topic/henry-ford

[30] Vance Havner. (n.d.). BrainyQuote.com. Retrieved November 11, 2011, from BrainyQuote.com Web site: http://www.brainyquote.com/quotes/quotes/v/vancehavne152363.html

[31] Murdock, Mike, The Assignment, Albury Publishing, Tulsa, Oklahoma 1997, pg 39

[32] C. S. Lewis. (n.d.). BrainyQuote.com. Retrieved November 11, 2011, from BrainyQuote.com Web site: http://www.brainyquote.com/quotes/quotes/c/cslewis131286.html

[33] Aristotle. (n.d.). Thinkexist.com. Retrieved May 18, 2011, from http://thinkexist.com/quotation/we_are_what_we_repeatedly_do-excellence_then-is/12820.html

[34] L.G. Elliott. (n.d.). MotivatingQuotes.com. Retrieved May 22, 2011, from http://www.motivatingquotes.com/habit.htm

[35] Ebenezer Scrooge. (2011, November 14). In Wikipedia, The Free Encyclopedia. Retrieved May 27, 2011, from http://en.wikipedia.org/w/index.php?title=Ebenezer_Scrooge&oldid=460525553

[36] Luke 16:19–31 New Living Translation **(NLT)** Holy Bible. New Living Translation copyright© 1996, 2004, 2007 by Tyndale House Foundation. Used by permission of Tyndale House Publishers Inc., Carol Stream, Illinois 60188

[37] Confucius. (n.d.). Quote Garden. Retrieved May 30, 2011, from http://www.quotegarden.com/habits.html

[38] Tryon Edwards. (n.d.). Thinkexist.com. Retrieved May 29, 2011, from http://thinkexist.com/quotes/tryon_edwards/

[39] Mark Twain. (n.d.). About.com. Retrieved May 31, 2011, from http://quotations.about.com/cs/inspirationquotes/a/Habits3.htm

[40] Edward Vernon Rickenbacker. (n.d.). Thinkexist.com. Retrieved Jun, 1, 2011, from http://thinkexist.com/quotes/edward_vernon_rickenbacker/

[41] Ralph Waldo Emerson. (n.d.). Thinkexist.com. Retrieved Jun, 5, 2011, from

Terminal Living

http://thinkexist.com/quotation/he_who_is_not_everyday_conquerin
g_some_fear_has/14505.html

Nelson Mandela. (n.d.). goodreads. Retrieved Jun 20, 2011, from
http://www.goodreads.com/author/quotes/367338.Nelson_Mandela

The King's Speech. (2011, November 15). In Wikipedia, The Free
Encyclopedia. Retrieved June 16, 2011, from
http://en.wikipedia.org/w/index.php?title=The_King%27s_Speech&
oldid=460852665443

Patrick Overton. (n.d.). Thinkexist.com. Retrieved June 23, 2011,
from http://thinkexist.com/quotes/patrick_overton/

Wayne Gretzky. (n.d.). Quote Garden. Retrieved June 11, 2011,
from http://www.quotegarden.com/risk.html

Secretariat (film). (2011, November 5). In Wikipedia, The Free
Encyclopedia. Retrieved June 16, 2011, from
http://en.wikipedia.org/w/index.php?title=Secretariat_(film)&oldid
=459201349

James Brian Conant. (n.d.). Quote Garden. Retrieved Jun 19,
2011, from
http://www.quotegarden.com/risk.html

Haugen, Gary A. Just Courage, Inter Varsity Press, Downers
Grove, IL, 2008, p. 120

Unknown. (n.d.). Thinkexist.com. Retrieved June 21, 2011, from
http://thinkexist.com/quotation/to_love_is_to_risk_not_being_loved
_in_return-to/9949.html

Theodore Roosevelt. (n.d.). BrainyQuote.com. Retrieved June 28,
2011, from BrainyQuote.com Web site:
http://www.brainyquote.com/quotes/quotes/t/theodorero109913.html

[51] Brandt, Paul. (2007). Risk Master. Risk. Giantfoothillbilly Music SOCAN. Retrieved May 10, 2011, from http://www.paulbrandt.com/content/music

[52] Stephen R Covey. (n.d.). Thinkexist.com. Retrieved June 15, 2011, from http://thinkexist.com/quotation/there_are_certain_things_that_are_fundamental_to/346905.html

[53] U.S. Fish and Wildlife Service. Pacific Salmon. Retrieved June 5, 2011, from http://www.fws.gov/species/species_accounts/bio_salm.html

[54] Anatole France. (2011, November 3). In Wikipedia, The Free Encyclopedia. Retrieved June 22, 2011, from http://en.wikipedia.org/w/index.php?title=Anatole_France&oldid=458772710

[55] Anatole France. (n.d.). BrainyQuote.com. Retrieved November 3, 2011, from BrainyQuote.com Web site: http://www.brainyquote.com/quotes/quotes/a/anatolefra104501.html

[56] Christine Gregoire. (n.d.). BrainyQuote.com. Retrieved June 22, 2011, from BrainyQuote.com Web site: http://www.brainyquote.com/quotes/quotes/c/christineg167885.html

[57] E. E. Cummings. (n.d.). Quote Garden. Retrieved June 18, 2011, from http://www.quotegarden.com/be-self.html

[58] Tommy Lasorda. (n.d.). Thinkexist.com. Retrieved June 14, 2011, from http://thinkexist.com/quotation/the_difference_between_the_impossible_and_the/225739.html

[59] Winston Churchill. (n.d.). Thinkexist.com. Retrieved June 23, 2011, from http://thinkexist.com/quotes/winston_churchill/

[60] Shmoop Editorial Team. (November 11, 2008).Maria W. Chapman in Abolitionists. Retrieved May 22, 2011, from http://www.shmoop.com/abolition/maria-w-chapman.html

[61] Maria W. Chapman. (n.d.). BrainyQuote.com. Retrieved June 4, 2011, from BrainyQuote.com Web site: http://www.brainyquote.com/quotes/quotes/m/mariawcha354715.html

[62] Scanlon, Paul, Crossing Over, Thomas Nelson, Nashville Tennessee, 2006, pg 153, 154

[63] Luke 2:49 King James Version **(KJV)** Public Domain

[64] John 19:30 New International Version **(NIV)** Copyright © 1973, 1978, 1984, 2011 by Biblica

[65] John 8:58 New International Version **(NIV)** Copyright © 1973, 1978, 1984, 2011 by Biblica

[66] John 10:18 Contemporary English Version **(CEV)** Copyright © 1995 by American Bible Society

[67] Matthew 27:22 New International Version **(NIV)** Copyright © 1973, 1978, 1984, 2011 by Biblica

[68] John 12:24–25 The Message **(MSG)** Copyright © 1993, 1994, 1995, 1996, 2000, 2001, 2002 by Eugene H. Peterson

[69] John 14:18–20 The Message **(MSG)** Copyright © 1993, 1994, 1995, 1996, 2000, 2001, 2002 by Eugene H. Peterson

[70] legacy. (n.d.). Dictionary.com Unabridged. Retrieved November 12, 2011, from Dictionary.com website: http://dictionary.reference.com/browse/legacy

[71] Terry Fox. (1979, October). Terry's letter. The Terry Fox Foundation. Retrieved May 1, 2011, from
http://www.terryfox.org/Foundation/Terrys_Letter.html

[72] Gaylord Nelson. (n.d.). Quotation Collection. Retrieved June 30, 2011, from
http://www.quotationcollection.com/author/Gaylord_Nelson/quotes

[73] William James. (n.d.). Quotation Collection. Retrieved June 28, 2011, from
http://www.quotationcollection.com/author/William_James/quotes

[74] Matthew 11:29–30 Contemporary English Version **(CEV)** Copyright © 1995 by American Bible Society

[75] John 10:10 Contemporary English Version **(CEV)** Copyright © 1995 by American Bible Society